BALTIC STATES
VS.
THE RUSSIAN EMPIRE

1000 Years of Struggle for Freedom

VAL RAMONIS

BALTIC STATES
VS.
THE RUSSIAN EMPIRE

1000 Years of Struggle for Freedom

Baltech Publishing
Lemont, Illinois
1991

Published by Baltech Publishing
P.O. Box 225
Lemont, Illinois 60439

Printed by Morkunas Printing Co., Chicago, Illinois
Cover printed by Questar Printing Co., Chicago, Illinois
Printed in the United States of America

Library of Congress Catalog Card Number: 91-72506

Cover: *Unarmed Lithuanian civilians try to push a tank away from a young woman being crushed to death. This is happening the night of "Bloody Sunday", during the brutal assault on the radio and television transmission tower in Vilnius, Lithuania by Soviet Interior Ministry special forces.*

Contents

Introduction

"Separatist factions in the tiny Baltic republics of Estonia, Latvia and Lithuania -- which were independent only a short period between the two World Wars -- are trying to secede from the Soviet Union".

This is a statement I have heard many times on television and radio or read in newspapers, and it makes me very upset. Upset not only because the statement is incorrect in its entirety, but because it shows that the press and the public are still unaware of what is really going on in that part of Europe.

The independence movements in the three Baltic States are not isolated manifestations by some "separatist factions". They are full-blown independence drives reflecting the wishes of the majority of the people in those countries. This was clearly demonstrated in the parliamentary elections of 1989 -- the first democratic elections held in the Baltics in 50 years -- where candidates running under the independence platforms won the majority of votes to the parliaments. It also was demonstrated by the plebiscites held in the Baltic States during February and March of 1991, by which over 75% of the Estonians and Latvians and more than 90% of the Lithuanians expressed their desire to be independent from the Soviet Union.

"Tiny Baltic republics" is another misconception. Tiny compared to what? To Russia? To Germany? To the United States? Of course.

But has anyone considered that Ireland, Switzerland, Holland, Belgium, Denmark, Luxembourg, Iceland and other European countries are either equal or smaller in size or population than the Baltic States? Does anyone refer to those countries as *"tiny"*?

Another part of the statement -- the one which refers to independence between the two World Wars -- is probably the one misunderstood the most. Although it's true that the three countries became modern independent states between 1918 and 1940, their independence was not limited to this short period.

Up until the 13th century, Estonia and Latvia enjoyed complete independence from foreign domination. From that time on, the two countries experienced periods of freedom, interspersed with brief occupations by Germans, Swedes, Poles, Lithuanians and Russians. Only in the 18th century -- during the Great Northern War between Sweden and Peter the Great of Russia -- would Estonia and Latvia finally succumb to the Russian Bear and loose their character as separate European entities.

Lithuania remained independent much longer. Up until the 16th century, the Lithuanian Kingdom -- later known as the Grand Duchy of Lithuania -- not only was a free and independent state, but a large and powerful one. Even though it united with Poland into a Commonwealth in 1569, it retained its sovereignty until 1795 when it was forcefully incorporated into the Russian Empire.

The last part of the statement, *"secede from the Soviet Union"* is incorrect as well. For a country to secede from another, it must have agreed to join it in the first place. In 1940 -- as in 1795 -- neither Lithuania, Latvia or Estonia agreed voluntarily to join Russia or the Soviet Union. They were forcefully invaded, occupied and annexed. Soviet President Mikhail Gorbachev's comparison of their incorporation into the Soviet Union to a marriage -- and their separation from the Union to a divorce -- is completely erroneous. There was no marriage, so there can be no divorce. The entire affair was more like a rape, with the three Baltic countries being the victims.

The purpose of this book is threefold. First, to present a brief description of 1000 years of confrontation between the Baltic nations and the Russian Empire, and its successor the U.S.S.R.; second, to dispel any misunderstanding that the public might have about the true origins, causes and reasons of the events occurring in the Baltic States today; and last, to correct the previously mentioned misconceptions in order to offer a truer picture of the Balts' aspirations and their quest for independence.

I hope this purpose has been achieved.

Val Ramonis

EAST
EUROPE

Miles
0   100   200   300

Beginnings of Confrontation

The problems facing Soviet leaders these days in their relations with the Baltic States of Estonia, Latvia and Lithuania are by no means new and shouldn't surprise them or anyone else familiar with Russian or Eastern European history. These problems are deep-rooted and are nothing more than a continuation of the conflicts which began in that part of Europe around the 10th century of our era between two ethnically and culturally distinct groups -- the Balts and the Slavs.

For thousands of years, the Balts had inhabited a huge expanse of land in northeastern Europe stretching from the Baltic Sea in the west to almost present-day Moscow in the east, and from Novgorod in the north to Kiev in the south. Their neighbors, the Fino-Ugrians, occupied a large area to their north.

The Slavs on the other hand, appeared on the scene around 500 A.D., absorbing or driving out the Balts and the Fino-Ugrians, and settling the region themselves. Consequently, the Balts were pushed into a smaller area that was to become Prussia, Latvia and Lithuania, and the Fino-Ugrians into present-day Estonia and Finland.

In the third quarter of the 9th century, the Slavic tribes were unified -- through force and coercion -- into a powerful state by the Varangians or Rus from Scandinavia, commonly called Vikings. The

11

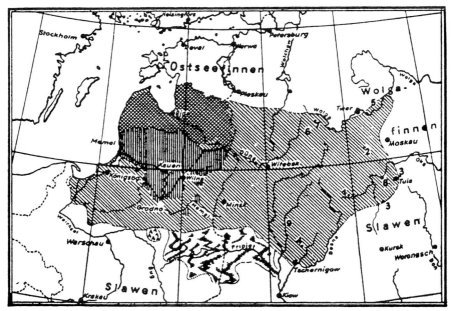

On this map of northeastern Europe, shaded areas indicate lands inhabited by the Balts prior to the arrival of the Slavs.

Rus were Swedish adventurers who had been using the abundant rivers of Eastern Europe for their trading and marauding expeditions with Constantinople and the Mediterranean, and who also built trading posts along the way. Gradually they controlled the entire country which became known as the "Land of the Rus", with Kiev and Novgorod as its capitals. Eventually this vast region would be called Kievan Russia, and later, just Russia.

As early as the 10th century -- and perhaps even earlier -- the Kievan and Novgorodian princes, successors of the Rus rulers, were already conducting military campaigns against their neighbors to the west, the Balts. The *Povest vremennych let chronicle* of 1113 records the raid of the first Christian Russian ruler, Prince Vladimir of Kiev

(980-1015), against the Lithuanians in 983. His son Yaroslav the Wise (1019-1054) did the same in 1038, 1040 and again in 1044. Attacks against the Estonians and Latvians began about the same time.

In essence, these campaigns were carried out as a retaliation for the incursions of the Balts into Russian territory, or for the purpose of obtaining booty and slaves. As the chronicles point out, the outcome of these adventures varied, sometimes with disastrous results for the Russians themselves.

By this time the Baltic peoples -- and particularly the Lithuanians -- were becoming militarily strong and showing signs of the beginnings of an organized political structure.

Throughout the 12th and up until the middle of the 13th centuries, the Balts themselves conducted a series of attacks against the Russian principalities of Novgorod and Pskov in the north, cities along the

Typical fortress of the Balts from the 10th-11th centuries.

Lithuanian warrior from the 11th-13th centuries. Dress and armament reconstructed from finds in burial sites.

Dnieper river in the east and points beyond the Pripet marshes in the south.

The Russians retaliated by raiding the Latvian province of Zemgale in 1106 and Lithuanian territories in 1113, 1132, 1203 and 1205. They even occupied southeastern Estonia in 1227. Then, suddenly, the Balto-Russian front came to a halt.

Out of the deep steppes of Asia, 150,000 Mongol warriors of the Golden Horde appeared, led by Batu, grandson of Genghis Khan. In a short period of only three years (1237-40), the Mongols devastated and subjugated all of Kievan Russia, with the exception of Novgorod, and threatened to overrun the lands inhabited by the Balts.

The *Lithuanian Chronicle* of the 16th century, the first written history of Lithuania, describes in minute detail how the Lithuanian hero Rimgaudas confronted a huge Mongol army at Mohilno on the banks of the upper Nemunas (Niemen) river in eastern Lithuania. He crushed the Mongol force in a fierce and decisive battle which put a stop to their drive westward, and possibly saved Western Europe from Mongol domination. It is mentioned in the *Lithuanian Chronicle* that in their attack against Baltic lands, the Mongols were aided by the princes of Kiev, Vladimir and Druck. It is not certain what motivated these Russian princes -- who themselves had been overrun by the Mongols a short time before -- to help their own oppressors in their attacks against the Balts.

Growth of Lithuania

A new era in Baltic-Russian relations began. Due to the oppression of the Russians by the Mongols, the balance of power in the region was tipping in favor of the Lithuanians. Around 1235, a pagan strongman by the name of Mindaugas rose above all other Lithuanian princes, accepted Christianity from Rome and was crowned as the first king of Lithuania.* He embarked on the task of consolidating all the Baltic lands under his domain, and to expand them even further by annexing neighboring territories inhabited by Slavs. In Mindaugas' as well as his successors' opinion, those lands belonged to the Balts because their ancestors had inhabited them since prehistoric times.

About the same time but farther north, the history of Estonia and Latvia was taking a different turn. Their problem was no longer the Russians but the crusading German Knights of the Teutonic Order, who had just arrived in their territory with the mission of converting

---

* It has become common practice to refer to Lithuanian rulers before and after Mindaugas as Grand Dukes. This title is not exactly accurate, as the rulers themselves never used it, nor were they called that way by others. It only came into use after the Lithuanian king Jogaila (Polish Jagiello) was also elected king of Poland in 1386, and his cousin Vytautas the Great took over the leadership of Lithuania with the title of Grand Duke.

In 1251 Mindaugas accepted Christianity and two years later was crowned as the first King of the Lithuanians. This historical event began Lithuanian statehood which is older than that of other countries of Europe. (From a painting by A. Varnas).

the last remaining European pagans to Christianity. As their brethren tried to do earlier in the Middle East, these crusaders finally managed to accomplish their task with fire and sword.

During the second half of the 13th century and the beginning of the 14th, a gradual Lithuanian expansion toward the south and the east began. Many Russian princes, whom the Mongols had conquered but had left in their old positions for the only purpose of collecting taxes from their subjects on their behalf, willingly surrendered themselves and their lands to the Lithuanian kings.

The replacement of Mongol by Lithuanian domination might appear but a small relief, but this was not at all the case. The

Lithuanians, though still mostly pagan, were rapidly mellowing and were tolerant of other people's religion, customs, culture and language. Russian nobles and boyars were treated as equals, and intermarriage was common; the Orthodox Church was respected, and many of the Lithuanian nobility became converts.

Mindaugas' successors Vytenis, Traidenis, Gediminas, Algirdas, Kestutis and particularly Vytautas the Great, expanded their territories eastward and southward to such extent that Lithuanians became a minority in their own country. In this huge empire were included the Russian principalities of Kiev, Polotsk, Smolensk, Chernigov and many others, and among its subjects were the White Russians and the Ukrainians. Gediminas (1316-41), who added Kiev to his dominions during one of his campaigns, called himself *"Rex*

The rulers of Kiev surrender the keys of their city to Gediminas. (From a 19th century engraving.)

19

Lithuanorum et Multorum Rusenorum" (King of Lithuanians and many Russians).

It is also worth mentioning that many of the acquisitions of Russian lands by the Lithuanian nobility occurred as a consequence of intermarriages and other social and political arrangements.

Although many large and small Russian principalities willingly accepted Lithuanian rule as opposed to that of the Mongols, a few others such as Muscovy, refused and resisted. This infuriated the Lithuanian king Algirdas (1345-77) so much that on three separate occasions, in 1368, 1370 and again in 1372, he attacked Muscovy and put siege to the Kremlin. Unable to take the fortress for the third

Algirdas with his armies outside the Kremlin walls. (From a painting by S. Usinskas.)

DID LIETUVOS KUNIGAIKSTIS
VYTAUTAS DIDYSIS
VIESPATAVO 1392-1430

Vytautas the Great (1392-1430), ruler of the Lithuanian Empire, is the most prominent personality in Lithuanian history. During his reign Lithuania became the most influential state in all of Europe. (From a painting by A. Varnas.)

time, Algirdas struck his sword against the Kremlin's gates and declared that he wouldn't leave until Prince Dimitri Ivanovich came out to discuss peace with him. The prince submitted to Algirdas' demand and signed a peace treaty with him. With the exception of the Mongol attack a hundred and thirty years earlier, this was the only time in history that someone had attacked Moscow and returned home undefeated.

Muscovy at the time was one of the smaller Russian principalities, but its influence over its neighbors was already beginning to be felt. Its growth as the dominant Russian principality did not begin until later, when its princes felt confident and strong enough to challenge the Mongol rule and refused to pay them tribute.

Algirdas' nephew Vytautas The Great (1392-1430), is regarded

Vytautas the Great with his legions on the shores of the Black Sea. (From a painting by J. Mackevicius.)

In 1429, Vytautas invited the rulers of Central and Eastern Europe to a peace conference. Sigismund, Emperor of the Holy Roman Empire, proposed that Vytautas be crowned King of Lithuania according to Western tradition. For all practical purposes, Vytautas was already a powerful king. (From a painting by S. Usinskas.)

as the supreme hero of the Lithuanian nation. He inherited an empire which in little more than one hundred years had increased twenty times its original size. He expanded it even further, pushing beyond Smolensk in the east and to the Crimea and the Black Sea in the south.

To consolidate his dominion over Russian lands even more, Vytautas arranged marriages between members of his family and Russian nobles. One of his daughters, Sofia, married Prince Vasily and became Grand Duchess of Muscovy. Although these strategies strengthened Lithuanian control over Russian lands at the time, they would backfire years later when Moscow's rulers try to regain them on the grounds that these areas belonged to them by right of inheritance.

At the time of Vytautas' death, Lithuania was the largest country in all of Europe, rivalling only the Holy Roman Empire in military strength and political influence.

The Empire of Vytautas the Great, stretching from the Baltic Sea to the Black Sea. (19th century map printed in Switzerland.)

24

The Threat from Moscow

Following the death of Vytautas, still another epoch in Baltic-Russian relations began. By 1480, Ivan III, Prince of Muscovy, whose ancestors in the 14th century received the title of Grand Prince of all Russia for their service to the Mongols as tax collectors, refused to pay them tribute, consolidated his strength and threw off the "Mongol Yoke". He also captured the cities of Pskov and Smolensk from the Lithuanians, Riazan from the Mongols, and made Moscow the center of all Russia.

Ivan III's expansionist policy was continued by his successors Vasily III (whose second wife was a Lithuanian princess) and Ivan IV the Terrible. By this time Lithuania had already evolved into such a strong military power, that it could not only repel Russian attacks, but also inflict serious damage in return. For example, at the Battle of Orsa near Smolensk, fought on September 8, 1514, a combined army of 25,000-30,000 Lithuanians and Poles led by the "Hetman" (Supreme Marshal of the Lithuanian Armies) Constantine Ostrogiskis defeated 80,000 Russians. A few years later, on January 26, 1564, at the Battle of Ula near Polotsk, an army of 5,000 Lithuanians, commanded by the "Hetman" Michael Radvilas (Radzivill) crushed 24,000-30,000 Russians. Neither Vasily III nor Ivan IV could get a peaceful night's sleep knowing that the Lithuanian army stood just across their western borders.

At the Battle of Orsa near Smolensk, 25,000-30,000 Lithuanians and Poles commanded by Constantine Ostrogiskis, defeated 80,000 Muscovites. (Woodcut from the *Bielski Chronicle* of 1597.)

Russian attacks during this time were not targeted against Lithuania alone, but also against Lithuania's neighbors to the north, the Estonians and Latvians. The German masters of Estonia and Latvia had exerted their control over the various local groups and had established the Livonian Confederacy which posed a threat to the Russians and prevented them access to the Baltic Sea. In 1557, during the so called Livonian War, the Russians succeeded in occupying large areas of Estonia and Latvia and destroying the Confederacy and

The rulers of Moscow humbly beg King Stephen Batory for peace through the intermediary of the Papal legate Possevini. (From a painting by J. Matejka.)

its political structure. Twenty five years later they were driven out by a combined Lithuanian-Polish army led by the young king Stephen Batory.

To better defend themselves against Russia's attacks and to check its further expansion westward, in 1569 Lithuania and Poland united into a Commonwealth by the Union of Lublin. Both countries were to be governed by a mutually elected monarch, but their armies, treasuries, code of laws and internal affairs would be independent of each other. In case of danger, one country would be obligated to provide assistance to the other. This Lithuanian-Polish Commonwealth should have been ready to move into the vacuum that was created when Mongol power declined in Russia, but now the Poles

Since ancient times Vilnius has been a bustling, cosmopolitan city with strong defensive walls, beautiful buildings and an active political, cultural, social and economic life. (From a 17th century engraving.)

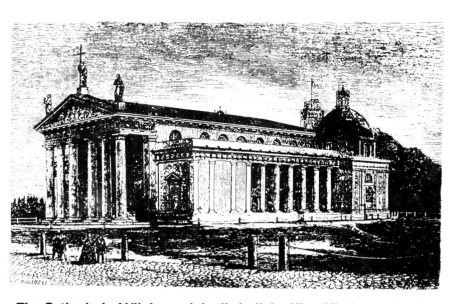

The Cathedral of Vilnius, originally built by King Mindaugas in the 13th century, was destroyed and rebuilt several times. The present Cathedral was designed by the Lithuanian architect Stuoka-Gucevicius and built between 1777 and 1801. After World War II, the communists took it away from the faithful and converted it into an art gallery and concert hall. Only in 1988 it was returned to the Lithuanians for religious use. (From a 19th century engraving.)

were engaged in fighting the Turks in the south, and their place was taken by the princes of Moscow.

Russia's drive into Baltic lands became so fierce from this time on, that in 1655, during his war with Sweden, Czar Aleksiej occupied most of Lithuania and captured Vilnius, its capital city for the first time. For two full days the Russians looted, burned and damaged so much of the city that the Czar had to camp in his own tent outside the city for lack of suitable accommodations. 14,000 people were killed; churches, palaces and most important buildings were destroyed, and art treasures, fine furnishings, even entire libraries were carted off to

Moscow. The Russians even dug up the tombs of Lithuanian kings and dignitaries searching for gold and jewels. Fortunately the inhabitants had hidden some of the remains, including those of Lithuania's patron Saint Casimir, before the Russians could get to them. The remains of Lithuania's most famous hero, Vytautas the Great, are still missing up to this day. It is not clear whether it was stolen by the Russians or was hidden from them and never found.

Six years after the Russians had captured Vilnius, the Lithuanian

Augustus III (1697-1733), King of the Lithuanian-Polish Commonwealth and Elector of Saxony. (From an 18th century engraving.)

"Hetman" Michael Pacas liberated the capital city and expelled the Russians from Lithuania.

While Lithuania, united with Poland, could withstand Russia's attacks and even counterattack, the Estonians and Latvians weren't as fortunate.

At the beginning of the 18th century, the Lithuanian-Polish Commonwealth was ruled by Augustus III, a German king from the House of Saxony, and the area of Estonia and Latvia -- which since medieval times had been referred to as Livonia -- was occupied by Sweden. Peter the Great's main concern was to give Russia access to the ice-free Baltic Sea. To that effect he conspired with the Lithuanian-Polish king, declared war on Sweden and during the so called Great Northern War, occupied Livonia. Estonia and Latvia would not see independence from Russian rule again until World War I.

From this time on, the Russian Czars began to meddle in the internal affairs of Lithuania and Poland. They created mistrust and friction between the king and the nobility, convinced the king to replace some of his local troops with Russians and even influenced the nobility to elect kings who were more sympathetic to the Czars than to their own subjects. One of these was Stanislav Augustus Poniatowski, who was to become the last king of Lithuania and Poland. He became Empress Catherine II the Great's favorite -- and some say lover -- whom she installed on the Lithuanian-Polish throne against the will of most and with the help of a few. As a result, an insurrection erupted against the king which was put down by Russian reinforcements sent by Catherine herself.

In 1772, Catherine's rivals, the kings of Austria and Prussia, in order to prevent her from taking over all the Lithuanian-Polish lands, convinced her to share parts of the Commonwealth with them. This action, which became known as the First Partition, gave each of the three monarchs sizeable chunks of Lithuanian and Polish territory.

Other similar partitions occurred in 1793 and again in 1795, the last one completely erasing Lithuania and Poland from the map of Europe for the next 123 years. Most of Lithuania fell under Russian control, with a smaller portion being taken by Prussia.

Under the Claw of the Czars

Following the occupation of Lithuania by the Russians, a period of russification and exploitation of the Lithuanian people began. Schools were either closed or turned into centers for the propagation of the Russian language. Churches, seminaries and convents were shut down. Freedom of religion only existed for the

A domiciliary visit by the Russian authorities in Lithuania. (19th century wood engraving from the *Illustrated London Times*.)

Russian Orthodox Church, which received lands and privileges from the government. The new rulers saw an opportunity to improve their social and financial status. The peasantry became taxed and oppressed as they had never been before. And young men were forcibly inducted into the Russian army, which meant long years of service in some remote Siberian outpost.

A bright streak of sunshine and hope appeared on the Lithuanian horizon when Napoleon decided to invade Russia in 1812. In his drive toward Moscow, Napoleon crossed the Lithuanian frontier unopposed and occupied Vilnius, Kaunas and other major cities. The Russian army and the local authorities fled ahead of Napoleon's advance, and the Lithuanian population flocked around him with offers of support in return for a promise of independence. Napoleon

Napoleon crosses the Nemunas river into Lithuania on his way to Moscow. (From a 19th century engraving by Couche.)

Insurgents lying in wait to intercept a Russian detachment. (19th century wood engraving from the *Illustrated London Times*.)

ladly accepted and got their support, military and otherwise, but promised nothing. After all, he hadn't become Emperor of most of Europe by granting independence to countries he had conquered, and he wasn't going to do it this time either. Napoleon's defeat in Russia snuffed out all hopes for Baltic independence, and the Czar's grip became even harsher.

Several revolts erupted in Lithuania and Poland against the Russians, notably in 1831 and 1863. As retribution for these insurrections, the Russian government closed the University of Vilnius and all other schools of higher learning, confiscated private land and other property, and hanged or deported to Siberia all those suspected guilty of participating in the revolts. In addition, in 1864 they

Dr. Vincas Kudirka (1858-1899), writer, publisher,
journalist, musician and a great patriot. He is the
author of the Lithuanian National Anthem.

instituted the infamous "Press Ban" in Lithuania by which the printing and even owning of books and periodicals printed in the Latin alphabet was strictly prohibited and harshly punishable.

In those days, as is still today in countries occupied by Russia, the outbreaks and revolts were a direct result of the ruthlessness of the occupiers and the innate desire of people to be free, coupled with deep periodic resurgences of national awareness. In the course of one hundred and twenty years in Lithuania, and almost two hundred years in Estonia and Latvia, the Russians used the harshest methods of repression in order to eradicate all forms of national and cultural identity and manifestation from these countries.

In their struggle to resist oppression, people became more astute in devising means and ways of circumventing the Russian authorities. When Russians forbade formal education of children in their native language, mothers taught children at home. When printing of books and newspapers in their language was prohibited, printing was done outside the country and books and newspapers were secretly brought in by book carriers called "knygnesiai" at great risk of their own lives. When priests and ministers were forbidden to teach religion or baptize children, they did so in secret.

These periods of tyranny and oppression gave birth to many brave and visionary men and women from all walks of life, who either with their words or their actions, defied the Russian authorities and awakened the national and cultural awareness of the people. These were the same men and women who at the outbreak of World War I and the Russian Revolution saw a ripe opportunity to break the chains of oppression and set themselves free again.

The Balts Regain Independence

1918 was a happy year for the Baltic countries. All three declared the restoration of their independence the same year, even though for all practical purposes they were not as yet free from foreign occupation. In 1915, while World War I was still raging, during its attack against Russia, Germany had invaded the Baltic countries, pushing the Russians out. Although Germany lost the war, in 1918 her army was still very much in control of the area. On

Young volunteers join the fledging Lithuanian army to fight for their country's independence.

Nutarimas.

Lietuvos Taryba savo posėdyje vasario 16 d. 1918 m. vienu balsu nu-
tarė kreiptis: į Rusijos, Vokietijos ir kitų valstybių vyriausybės šiuo
pareiškimu:

Lietuvos Taryba, vienintelė lietuvių tautos atstovybė, remdamos
pripažintaja tautų apsisprendimo teise ir lietuvių Vilniaus konferencijos
nutarimu rugsėjo mėn. 18-23 d. 1917 metais, skelbia atstatanti nepriklausomą demokratiniais pamatais sutvarkytą Lietuvos valstybę su sostine
Vilniuje ir tą valstybę atskirianti nuo visų valstybiniu ryšiu, kurie
yra buvę su kitomis tautomis.

Drauge Lietuvos Taryba pareiškia, kad Lietuvos valstybės pama-
tus ir jos santykius su kitomis valstybėmis privalo galutinai nustatyti
kiek galima graičiau sušauktas steigiamasis seimas, demokratiniu budu
visu jos gyventojų išrinktas.

Lietuvos Taryba pranešdama apie tai ....
vyriausybei, prašo pripažinti nepriklausomą Lietuvos valstybę.

Vilniuje, vasario 16 d. 1918 m.

Lithuania's Declaration of Independence.

RESOLUTION

The Council of Lithuania in its meeting on February 16, 1918, voted unanimously to address the governments of Russia, Germany, and other states with the following declaration:

The Council of Lithuania, as a sole representative of the Lithuanian people, on the basis of the recognized right of self-determination of nations and of the decision of the Lithuanian Conference in Vilnius, September 18-23, 1917, hereby proclaims the restoration of an independent, democratically organized Lithuanian State, with Vilnius its capital, and the abolition of all political ties which have existed with other nations.

The Council of Lithuania also declares that the foundation of the Lithuanian State and its relations with other countries must be finally determined by a Constituent Assembly, democratically elected by all the inhabitants of Lithuania.

The Council of Lithuania in informing the government of........ (the country addressed) requests recognition of the Independent State of Lithuania.

Vilnius, February 16, 1918

Signed by the members of the Council

Dr. J. Basanavicius	A. Petrulis
S. Banaitis	K. Saulys
M. Birziska	Dr. J. Saulys
K. Bizauskas	J. Sernas
P. Dovydaitis	A. Smetona
S. Kairys	J. Smilgevicius
P. Klimas	J. Staugaitis
D. Malinauskas	A. Stulginskis
V. Mironas	J. Vailokaitis
S. Narutavicius	J. Vileisis

Lithuania's Declaration of Independence (English translation).

41

February 16th of that year -- and in defiance of the German High Command -- Lithuanians proclaimed the restoration of their independence. On February 24th the Estonians did the same, and on November 18th, the Latvians. Under pressure from all sides, the German army was forced to abandon its occupied lands.

The newly installed Bolshevik government in Moscow hurried its army to the area to replace the void left by the retreating Germans. The Bolshevik forces managed to occupy some areas for a while, and to even set up local puppet governments with the purpose of forcing the three countries to return to Mother Russia. But their efforts were fruitless. The newly independent republics elected their own democratic governments who mustered inexperienced and poorly

Lithuanian soldiers with captured Bolshevik armament.

Vilnius, ancient capital of Lithuania, city of art and beautiful architecture. Most of the churches seen here were closed down by the Soviets and converted into warehouses, factories, museums, concert halls and even communist party offices. (Pre-World War II photograph.)

armed, but sizeable volunteer armies, and succeeded in expelling the invaders. It must have been a great blow to Lenin's pride.

The Western powers, winners in the Great War, watched these events with great interest. Some, like England, Finland, Sweden and Denmark supported the newly emerged republics and even provided military assistance in their fight to expel the Bolsheviks and the remains of the German army. Others felt that Russia had every right to regain its former possessions. They did not wish to antagonize the new Russian leaders and some countries even created obstacles to prevent the Balts from attaining their independence.

On July 12, 1920, the governments of the Republic of Lithuania

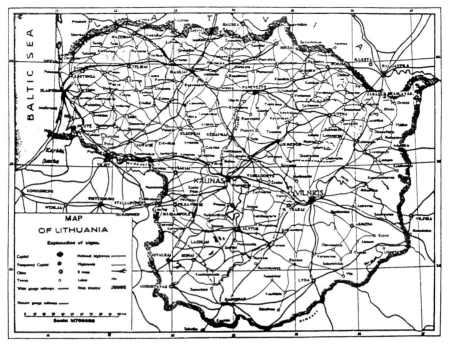

Map of the Republic of Lithuania showing borders that were agreed upon in 1920 by the governments of Lithuania and Soviet Russia. That same year Lenin renounced claims to all three Baltic countries for all time.

and the Russian Socialist Federated Soviet Republic, signed a peace treaty in Moscow by which Lenin renounced all claims to Lithuanian territory for all time. Similar treaties were signed with Estonia and Latvia on February 2, 1920, and August 11, 1920, respectively. In 1926, Lithuania and the Soviet Union signed a mutual Amity and Non-Aggression Pact, which was renewed in 1934, and was to be extended to December 31, 1941.

During the twenty two years following the restoration of their independence, the three Baltic republics experienced such progress and freedom as they hadn't for a long time. All three became members of the League of Nations, established diplomatic relations with most countries, their teams competed in World Olympics, their products were praised at World Fairs. Industry, trade and commerce were booming. Their currencies were strong, their governments stable. Their economies, culture and standards of living were catching up to the rest of the free world after being suppressed and degraded by hundreds of years of foreign occupation. Then suddenly, once again, everything ended.

The Baltic Holocaust Begins

On August 23, 1939, the Soviet Union and Nazi Germany signed the infamous secret Non-Aggression treaty known as the Molotov-Ribbentrop Pact by which Eastern Europe was divided into separate "spheres of influence". The Soviet Union was

Stalin shakes the hand of German Foreign Minister Ribbentrop after the conclusion of the Soviet-Nazi Pact on September 28, 1939.

In July 1940, Moscow installed a puppet communist government in Lithuania.

to receive the Baltic states and part of Poland in exchange for Stalin's guarantee of non-interference in Hitler's affairs. Without much advance warning or formal declaration of war, during June 15-17, 1940, the Red Army occupied the three countries. All previous peace treaties and non-aggression pacts were blatantly broken by the Soviets. About a month and a half later, rigged elections were staged in all three countries. As a result of those elections, in which only 10-15% of the population participated, all three were forcibly incorporated into the Union of Soviet Socialist Republics as its newest members.

Soviet leaders hadn't forgiven the Balts for separating from Russia in 1918. Between June 1940 and June 1941, and particularly during June 14-15, 1941, hundreds of thousands of innocent Estonians, Latvians and Lithuanians -- men, women, old folks and children, even newborn babies -- were rounded up in boxcars and deported to the Siberian wilderness to die in forced labor camps from unbearable cold and starvation. Tens of thousands of others from all walks of life were imprisoned, tortured or murdered without reason. In a short period of one year, the Baltic states lost about a fourth of their total population. Only Hitler's attack on Russia in June of 1941 prevented the complete annihilation of Baltic civilization.

The chance to liberate themselves presented once more to the Balts when Hitler double-crossed and attacked his former ally. During the short period between the retreat of the Russians and the arrival of the Germans, the Balts took up arms, regained control of

In June 1941, retreating Russians massacred over 400 political prisoners at the Pravieniskiai hard-labor camp in Lithuania.

their main cities, elected their own free governments, proclaimed the re-establishment of their independent states and began putting things back in order. But the uprisings were swiftly put down by the Germans, and the hope for independence was once again suffocated. A new period of occupation, repression and persecutions began under the Nazis, costing the Balts hundreds of thousands of additional lives. This terror lasted until 1944, when it was replaced by the second Soviet occupation.

In their push toward Berlin, the advancing Red Army expelled the Germans and regained control of the Baltic states for the second time in four years. The 1940 status of Soviet republics was re-established in all three countries. Puppet communist governments loyal to Moscow were again installed, civil liberties and human rights abolished, and once more innocent people were put in prisons or deported to Siberia for no more reason than before.

Slavery Again

I t is estimated that between 1945 and 1955, several hundred thousand Estonians, Latvians and Lithuanians were shipped off to Siberian death camps. As an example, from the Latvian provinces of Vidzeme and Latgala alone, 50,000 people were exiled to Siberia in only one year. Private land and all personal property was confiscated again and farmers were forced into collective farms.

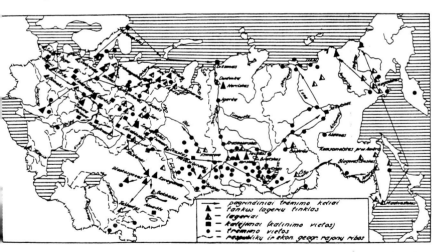

Map of the Soviet Union pinpoints locations of prisons and death camps to which Estonians, Latvians, Lithuanians and other nationalities were deported following the takeover of their countries by the Soviets.

51

In this photo taken at a Siberian forced-labor camp, deportees mourn the death of a dear relative. Their living quarters can be seen on the right.

The slightest criticism of the Soviet system was considered antirevolutionary and a serious crime. The display of pre-occupation era symbols such as national flags, state emblems or national anthems was a serious offense against the State, punishable by prison, deportation, and even death. A strong movement of armed partisan resistance began, especially in Lithuania, which fought the occupation for almost ten years. This resistance succeeded in inflicting heavy casualties to the Red Army, the NKVD (predecessor of the KGB) and the local communist officials and collaborators. Finally, poorly armed, hungry and exhausted, with casualties mounting and without hope of winning or receiving outside help, the partisans ended their activities.

This monument dedicated to the memory of those who died
for Lithuania's freedom -- erected after Lithuania regained
its independence in 1918 -- is one of thousands of
monuments and shrines demolished by the Soviets after
their takeover of the Baltic States.

Armed opposition to Soviet occupation was replaced by a different, non-violent, underground resistance which continued intermittently until recently. Because of this resistance, thousands -- perhaps even tens of thousands of people -- suffered cruel persecution, incarceration, forced internment into psychiatric hospitals and exile to Siberia.

Many clandestine opposition newspapers, called "samizdat", began to be published and circulated by anonymous writers, editors, publishers and printers under the harshest of conditions and at great risks to their lives. These newspapers, such as the *Chronicle of the Catholic Church of Lithuania* for example, reported the atrocities committed by the communists, and helped keep the fires of freedom alive in the hearts and minds of the people. Countless individuals suffered severely as a result of printing, distributing or even possessing copies of this type of literature. Beginning with the second Soviet Russian occupation, a systematic process of russification, colonization and exploitation of the Baltic republics was implemented, not unlike the one in effect during the Czarist occupation. The native languages were denigrated and relegated to secondary status while Russian was instituted as the official language in all republics. Centuries-old historical and traditional names of streets, squares, even of cities and towns were changed to foreign sounding names glorifying Russian heroes or communist accomplishments. National monuments, landmarks and shrines were either destroyed, left neglected to deteriorate or were turned into factories or warehouses.

Religious activity of any kind was forbidden or restricted to the minimum. Countless parishes were left unattended since only a very small number of priests or ministers were allowed to be ordained each year. No religious literature of any type was permitted to be printed and many houses of worship were closed down or taken away from the parishioners to be converted to other uses. A good example is the

A. Terleckas   V. Skuodis   A. Statkevičius

G. Iešmantas   P. Pečeliūnas   J. Sasnauskas

G. Navickaitė   O. Vitkauskaitė   A. Janulis

These are only a few of the thousands who suffered persecution, repression and harsh punishment at the hands of the Soviet authorities for their patriotic activities and struggle for human rights. As a result of changes that occurred throughout the Soviet Union during 1988 and 1989, they were realeased from prison or were allowed to return from Siberian exile.

Cathedral of Vilnius, where the remains of their patron Saint Casimir, Vytautas the Great and many other Lithuanian kings and heroes were buried. This, perhaps the holiest shrine in all of Lithuania, was turned into an art gallery and concert hall after the occupation. Only in 1989, by taking advantage of a more relaxed Soviet attitude toward religion, the Lithuanian faithful demanded and got from the local communist authorities the return of the Cathedral for its originally intended use. The remains of their patron saint were also returned to their original resting place.

National customs and traditions were curtailed or modified to fit Soviet standards. Holidays such as Christmas, Easter, St. Casimir's Day or Independence Day were abolished and replaced by communist holidays. It was said that if you were born on Christmas Day or on one of the other banned holidays, you could be prosecuted for celebrating your own birthday on that particular day.

Another form of russification and colonization tactic implemented by the Soviets was to shift the inhabitants of one republic to another far away in order to mix people of diverse ethnic cultures, thus diluting the local native population. Balts were forcibly moved to the interior of Russia or to one of the Asian republics, and similarly, Russians, Ukrainians, Byelorussians, even Asians were transplanted into the Baltic states. This way, in the course of 50 years, Estonia lost 40% of its native population, Latvia 50% and Lithuania 20%. These losses were replaced by colonists brought in from other, mostly Slavic republics.

National Rebirth

Now comes the era of *Glasnost* and *Perestroika* into the picture. When Gorbachev designed his policies of restructuring and openness, he was thinking primarily of economic reforms for a bankrupt Soviet system which could not catch up with or even follow the rest of the civilized world. Although the Soviets had made great inroads in space exploration and arms development, their economic situation at the consumer level was, as it is today, in shambles.

The Baltics, being the most western and the most economically advanced of all Soviet republics, were to be used by Gorbachev as guinea pigs for the experiment of his new economic policies. All three are small and somewhat distant from the center of the Soviet Union. If something did go wrong, they could be easily isolated from the rest of the country and reverted back to their original condition.

What Gorbachev failed to predict is that by allowing economic reforms in the Baltics, he also was putting in motion the wheels of political reforms that continue to turn at a faster rate every day. What originally began as a demand for more economic freedoms from Moscow, turned into demands for more political autonomy, even outright independence from the Soviet Union.

Under the old regimes prior to Gorbachev, any dissention or

Massive demonstrations, such as this one organized by the
Lithuanian reform movement *Sajudis* in June 1988, are typical of
the manifestations expressed by people in all three Baltic republics
demanding independence from the Kremlin. (Photograph by
Andrius Petrulevicius.)

patriotic manifestation was considered anti-revolutionary and
punishable as a crime against the state. With the coming of Gorbachev, the dissidents reversed the situation and accused anyone who
interfered with their demands for reforms or independence as being
Stalinist and anti-Perestroika.

A great number of reform movements and patriotic organizations
sprung up in the three republics since 1988. Some of these groups
had been working in the underground for quite some time, but until
recently did not dare to come out in the open.

Many of the national and patriotic organizations that existed in the prewar independence days such as scouts, student organizations, even old political parties, were revived and continue to be revived. Many others were created from scratch. Some, like the *Sajudis* movement in Lithuania for example, counted their followers in the hundreds of thousands, although they never referred to them as members. They did so to avoid being labeled a political party, thus preventing direct confrontation with Moscow.

Much was accomplished by these reform organizations and movements during those critical years. Local communist authorities, even Moscow itself, agreed to some of their demands, although not to all. Pre-war flags, anthems and other national symbols were

A line of armed Soviet militia gets ready to disperse a peaceful Lithuanian demonstration in Vilnius on September 28, 1988. (Photograph by Andrius Petrulevicius.)

allowed to be used by some of the republics. Most prisoners of conscience were released from jails or Siberian labor camps.

Travel restrictions to the west were eased somewhat, although anyone travelling to or from anywhere in the Soviet Union still had to go through Moscow and submit to the most lengthy and troublesome scrutiny by Soviet customs agents. Recently flights have been initiated into the Baltics from Berlin, Stockholm and other European cities, thus bypassing Moscow. But the Soviets still control the issuance of visas and passports as well as the customs offices.

The native languages, which for fifty years were relegated to secondary status and were constantly denigrated, were reinstated in the Baltic republics. Some churches were·returned to their rightful

A youth waving the flag of Independent Lithuania confronts the Soviet militia during a pro-independence rally in Vilnius.

Two views of the Lithuanian Statue of Liberty. The one on the left
was removed by the Soviets upon their occupation of Lithuania in
1940. The other one was reconstructed and rededicated on February
16th, 1989, in commemoration of the 71st anniversary of Lithuanian
independence.

owners -- the faithful, and a few were allowed to be repaired by the parishioners. One or two were even permitted to be built, the first churches to be built east of Poland since World War II.

An overall atmosphere of national rebirth was evident everywhere. People were no longer afraid to talk, to assemble, even to demonstrate, although they did not forget that big brother was still watching them, and that things could change overnight. Demonstrations for outright independence in the Baltics became almost a weekly occurrence. Manifestations such as the 1989 Baltic Way -- a chain of hands through the three republics in which over a million people participated -- attracted not only the attention of Soviet leaders and press, but of the entire world as well. Front page stories in both the American and international press covered these events extensively.

We all have watched the events unfolding in the Baltic states during the last few years. Those events have truly been staggering. First, Estonia's Parliament declared that it would not obey Soviet laws if those laws conflicted with Estonia's interests. Next, the Lithuanian Parliament denounced as illegal the annexation of Lithuania to the Soviet Union in 1940, and labeled it an international crime. A few days later the same Parliament abolished article 6 from the constitution of the Lithuanian republic, allowing a multi-party system and putting an end to communist party monopoly. Afterwards, the Lithuanian communist party separated itself from the central party in Moscow, prompting Gorbachev to go to Lithuania with hopes of mending the rift. He returned home unsuccessful.

Multi-party elections to the Parliament of Lithuania, the first in almost 50 years, were held in February 1990. The candidates supported by *Sajudis* -- running on a platform of Lithuanian independence -- won the majority of seats in the Parliament, while the hard-line communists supported by Moscow lost. Suddenly, a few days later, on March 11, the Lithuanians decided it was time to act.

Dr. Vytautas Landsbergis, President of the Republic of Lithuania.

In an unprecedented move the Lithuanian Parliament declared the restoration of Lithuania's independence and of the Lithuanian State as it existed prior to 1940. The Parliament elected *Sajudis* leader and musicologist Vytautas Landsbergis as the new President of the Republic of Lithuania. Immediately, Landsbergis selected his Cabinet of Ministers with Kazimiera Prunskiene as the Premier. New laws were enacted and the government set forth on the path of rebuilding the newly restored democracy.

But things never go as smoothly as one would like to anticipate. As soon as Lithuania declared its independence, the world, the Kremlin and most of all Mikhail Gorbachev were stunned. A period of calm and deadly silence followed. Suddenly, without warning, this silence was broken by Red Army tanks and armored personnel carriers rumbling through the streets of Vilnius. The worst was expected, perhaps another massacre similar to the one in Hungary in 1956 or Czechoslovakia in 1968. Fortunately the massacre did not materialize at that time. But Gorbachev did show his discontent by ordering army units to occupy public buildings in Lithuania, to beat up Lithuanian deserters who had been illegally inducted into the Soviet Army and were seeking refuge in Red Cross hospitals, to scare Lithuanians into submission by sending Migs and helicopters flying over Vilnius, and to demand that all hunting and sporting weapons be handed over to the army. These tactics did not work and Lithuanians stood firm in their position.

The Estonians and Latvians followed the Lithuanians in asserting their desire to seek independence from the Kremlin as well, although they decided to go about it more carefully. On May 4, Latvia dropped the "Soviet" from its name and became the Republic of Latvia. Days later Estonia did the same.

Gorbachev decided to employ a different tactic to submit Lithuanians into rescinding their declaration of independence. An

Symbols of Soviet rule in the Baltics.

economic, political and cultural blockade of Lithuania was imposed the following August, causing millions of dollars worth of damage to the country's economy and enormous hardship to the people. The embargo was finally lifted after the Lithuanians agreed to impose a moratorium on their March 11 declaration in exchange for independence talks with Moscow.

Gorbachev didn't seem willing to talk about independence for the Baltic States, or any of the other 12 republics. He wanted to keep the Soviet Union intact and didn't want to go down in history as the Soviet leader who permitted its collapse. His actions, such as requesting excessive presidential powers and bringing communist, Red Army and KGB hard-liners into his government, testified to this.

January 13, 1991 will always be remembered in Lithuania as "Bloody Sunday". On that tragic day and without any provocation, Soviet Interior Ministry troops and paratroopers, aided by local communists, attacked the Vilnius communications center housing Lithuania's television and radio studios. In a brutal assault with tanks and armored vehicles, the Soviets murdered 14 unarmed civilian defenders -- including women, teenagers and the elderly -- and wounded more than 500, many of them seriously. A week later, Soviet troops continued their rampage by attacking the Interior Ministry building in Riga, Latvia, killing 5 civilians including a reporter filming the incident. These actions were nothing more than another step in the repression of freedom in the Baltics. Although Gorbachev denied he had anything to do with these assaults, not many believed him. He was the country's president and the Commander in Chief of the Army and all responsibility for the killings was his. Up to this day no one has been brought to trial for these murders. As a matter of fact, on June 2, 1991, the Soviet chief prosecutor issued a statement blaming Lithuanian authorities for the killings. He said Lithuanians fired at each other and pushed their friends in front of

A childrens' book publisher struggles with an armed Soviet paratrooper trying to take his camera away and prevent the recording of "Bloody Sunday" in Vilnius.

anks as a publicity stunt to attract sympathy for the independence movement.

On February 9, 1991, the Lithuanian people had the opportunity to show the entire world -- and Gorbachev in particular -- what they thought of his proposed new union treaty, and to express once again their desire to become a free nation. In a nationwide referendum where 80% of all eligible voters participated, 90.5% answered yes to the question "Do you believe that Lithuania should be an independent democratic republic?"

On March 1, Estonia and Latvia held similar referendums, and even though the native ethnic population in these republics is only

Signs such as these express the feelings of the Balts towards their occupiers. (Photo by Andrius Petrulevicius).

slightly more than half of the total population, the results were just as astonishing (over 75% in both countries).

Intimidations and open aggression by the Kremlin did not subside after the January massacres in Vilnius and Riga. Soviet Interior Ministry "Black Beret" troops continued their campaign of terror by attacking and burning dozens of customs post along the Lithuanian and Latvian borders. Several unarmed guards were killed and many injured in these unprovoked attacks. The Soviet Interior Ministry denied any implication in these incidents, and Boris Pugo, the Interior Minister, said he had no knowledge of any such attacks. In June the aggression escalated in Lithuania when a unit of the "Black Berets" -- under the pretext of a weapons search -- assaulted the Vilnius central telephone exchange building, interrupting telecommunications throughout Lithuania and cutting the country off from the rest of the world for several hours. Fortunately there were no casualties this time.

On July 10, an incredible thing -- a first in the 1000-year history of the Russian Empire -- occurred. On that particular day, Boris Yeltsin, a reformer democrat and Mikhail Gorbachev's chief rival, was inaugurated as the first freely and popularly elected leader of the Russian Federation, the largest and most populous of the Soviet republics. Yeltsin's election as president of Russia was not only a victory for democracy, but a defeat for Gorbachev and the communist party as well.

Yeltsin's victory did not deter the Soviet Interior Ministry from further attacks. On July 30, while President Bush was in Moscow signing the Strategic Arms Treaty with Gorbachev, "Black Berrets" massacred 7 Lithuanian officials at the Medininkai customs post on the Lithuanian-Byelorussian border.

The three Baltic States have never experienced such world-wide attention and exposure in the mass media -- not even during World War II when the Red Army invaded them for the first time. And this trend doesn't seem to be subsiding. These are three courageous countries whose residents still remember their pre-World War II independence days.

By observing the events of the last few years, one can deduct with certainty that the Balts will not stop their efforts until those days are back again. And unless the Kremlin leaders learn a lesson from past history and abandon their policy of aggression, oppression and illegal occupation of neighboring countries, their troubles with the Baltics will continue.

EXTRA   EXTRA   EXTRA

As this book was going to print, events of cataclysmic proportions shook the Soviet Union and reverberated throughout the world. These events grew in scope and intensity by the hour.

On August 19, while Gorbachev was vacationing in the Crimea, a group of hard-liners headed by Soviet Vice-President Gennadi Yanayev assumed control of the government in a poorly planned coup d'etat. Gorbachev was put under house arrest. The plotters, backed by the communist party, the KGB and some army generals, took control of key positions in Moscow and in the Baltics. But they underestimated the people who stood up against the plotters and prevented them from capturing Yeltsin and the Russian Parliament. Some army units joined Yeltsin while others refused to shoot civilians and turned back. Three days later the coup collapsed and its perpetrators were captured or dead. Gorbachev returned to his post with greatly diminished powers and Yeltsin became the supreme hero.

While the coup was in progress, Estonia declared the restoration of its full independence on August 20, and Latvia the following day. The failure of the coup gave rise to a chain of events unparalleled in Russian history. Statues of Lenin and other communist heroes were toppled in Moscow and throughout the republics. The communist party was banned for its participation in the coup. The KGB was stripped of its powers and privileges. Anyone suspected of supporting the conspirators -- including many high-ranking military officers -- was imprisoned, fired or replaced. Others took their own lives.

In the Baltics, buildings seized and occupied by the Soviets were returned. Activities of the communists and the KGB were banned and each country took control of its borders. By the end of August, scores of countries around the world -- including the U.S. and the entire European Community -- had recognized Baltic independence.

70

Appendix

LIETUVOS RESPUBLIKOS AUKŠČIAUSIOSIOS TARYBOS

A K T A S

DĖL LIETUVOS NEPRIKLAUSOMOS VALSTYBĖS ATSTATYMO

Lietuvos Respublikos Aukščiausioji Taryba, reikšdama Tautos valią, nutaria ir iškilmingai skelbia, kad yra atstatomas 1940 metais svetimos jėgos panaikintas Lietuvos Valstybės suvereninių galių vykdymas, ir nuo šiol Lietuva vėl yra nepriklausoma valstybė.

Lietuvos Tarybos 1918 m. vasario 16 d. Nepriklausomybės aktas ir 1920 m. gegužės 15 d. Steigiamojo Seimo rezoliucija dėl atstatytos Lietuvos demokratinės valstybės niekada nebuvo nustoję teisinės galios ir yra Lietuvos Valstybės konstitucinis pamatas.

Lietuvos valstybės teritorija yra vientisa ir nedaloma, joje neveikia jokios kitos valstybės konstitucija.

Lietuvos valstybė pabrėžia savo ištikimybę visuotinai pripažintiems tarptautinės teisės principams, pripažįsta sienų neliečiamumą, kaip jis suformuluotas 1975 metų Europos saugumo ir bendradarbiavimo pasitarimo Helsinkyje Baigiamajame akte, garantuoja žmogaus, piliečio ir tautinių bendrijų teises.

Lietuvos Respublikos Aukščiausioji Taryba kaip suvereninių galių reiškėja šiuo aktu pradeda realizuoti visą Valstybės suverenitetą.

LIETUVOS RESPUBLIKOS
AUKŠČIAUSIOSIOS TARYBOS PIRMININKAS

V. LANDSBERGIS

LIETUVOS RESPUBLIKOS
AUKŠČIAUSIOSIOS TARYBOS SEKRETORIUS

L. SABUTIS

Vilnius, 1990 m. kovo 11 d.

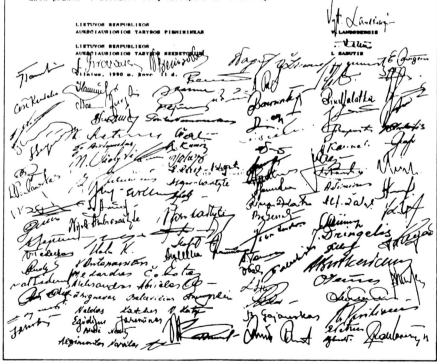

Act on the Restoration of the Lithuanian State.

SUPREME COUNCIL OF THE REPUBLIC OF LITHUANIA

ACT ON THE RESTORATION OF THE LITHUANIAN STATE

The Supreme Council of the Republic of Lithuania, expressing the will of the Nation, resolves and solemnly proclaims that the execution of the sovereign power of the Lithuanian State, heretofore constrained by alien forces in 1940, is restored, and henceforth Lithuania is once again an independent state.

The February 16, 1918, Act of Independence of the Supreme Council of Lithuania and the May 16, 1920, Constituent Assembly Resolution on the restoration of a democratic Lithuanian State have never lost their legal force and are the constitutional foundations of the Lithuanian State.

The territory of Lithuania is integral and indivisible, and the Constitution of any other state has no jurisdiction within it.

The Lithuanian State emphasizes its adherence to universally recognized principles of international law, recognizes the principle of inviolability of borders as formulated in Helsinki in 1976 in the Final Act of the Conference on Security and Cooperation in Europe, and guarantees rights of individuals, citizens and ethnic communities.

The Supreme Council of the Republic of Lithuania, expressing sovereign power, by this act begins to achieve the State's full sovereignty.

Vytautas Landsbergis
Chairman of the Supreme Council
of the Republic of Lithuania

Liudvikas Sabutis
Secretary of the Supreme Council
of the Republic of Lithuania

Vilnius, March 11, 1990

Signed by all the members of the Supreme Council (Parliament)

Act on the Restoration of the Lithuanian State (English translation.)

Defenders of the Vilnius radio and television transmission tower killed by Soviet troops on "Bloody Sunday". From the top, first row: Loreta Asanaviciute, Darius Gerbutavicius; second row: Vidas Maciulevicius, Vytautas Vaitkus, Rimantas Juknevicius; third row: Alvydas Matulka, Rolandas Jankauskas, Apolinaras Povilaitis, Titas Masiulis; fourth row: Alvydas Kanapinskas, Algimantas Kavaliukas, Ignas Simulionis, Vytautas Koncevicius, Virginijus Druskis.

Suggestions for Further Reading

Bourdeaux, Michael, *Land of Crosses*, Devon, 1980

Brogan, Patrick, *The Captive Nations - Eastern Europe 1945-1990*, New York, 1990

Budreckis, A., *Lithuanian National Revolt of 1941*, Boston, 1968

Chase, Thomas G., *The Story of Lithuania*, New York, 1946

Dauknys, Pranas, *The Resistance of the Catholic Church in Lithuania Against Religious Persecution*, Rome, 1981

Daumantas, Juozas, *Fighters for Freedom: Lithuanian Partisans Versus the U.S.S.R.*, Toronto, 1975

Gerutis, Albert (editor), *Lithuania: 700 Years*, New York, 1969

Gimbutas, Marija, *The Balts*, London, 1963

Harrison, Ernst J., *Lithuania's Fight for Freedom*, New York, 1952

Jurgela, Constantine P., *History of the Lithuanian Nation*, New York, 1948

Jusaitis, Antanas, *The Story of Lithuania*, Philadelphia, 1918

Kaslas, Bronis J. (editor), *The U.S.S.R.-German Aggression Against Lithuania, a Documentary History 1939-1945*, New York, 1973

Koncevicius, Joseph B., *Russia's Attitude Towards Union with Rome (9th-16th Centuries)*, Washington, 1927

Koncius, Joseph B., *Vytautas the Great, Grand Duke of Lithuania*, Miami, 1964

Krepp, E., *The Baltic States*, Stockholm, 1968

Lithuanian National Foundation, Inc. (publisher), *Memorandum on the Restoration of Lithuania's Independence, 1988*

Manning, Clarence A., *The Forgotten Republics*, New York, 1952

Mantenieks, Maris (editor), *The Baltic States - Yesterday Forgotten ... Remembered Today*, Lakewood, Ohio

Mazeika, Rasa, Dr. (editor), *Violations of Human Rights in Soviet Occupied Lithuania: A Report for 1983-1986*, Philadelphia, 1988

Misiunas, Romuald, J. & Taagepera, Rein, *The Baltic States: The Years of Dependence*, Berkeley, 1983

Norem, Owen J.C., Dr., *Timeless Lithuania*, Chicago, 1943

Norus, T. and Zilius J., *Lithuania's Case for Independence*, Washington, 1918

Page, Stanley W., *The Formation of the Baltic States*, Cambridge, 1959

Pajaujis-Javis, Joseph, Ph.D., *Soviet Genocide in Lithuania*, New York, 1980

Paszkiewicz, Henryk, *The Origin of Russia*, London, 1954

Payne, Robert & Romanoff, Nikita, *Ivan the Terrible*, New York, 1975

Pick, D.W., *The Baltic Nations*, London, 1945

Pusta, K.R., *The Soviet Union and the Baltic States*, New York, 1943

Raun, Toivo, *Estonia and the Estonians*, Stanford, 1987

Read, Anthony and Fisher, David, *The Deadly Embrace: Hitler, Stalin and the Nazi-Soviet Pact of 1939-41*, New York, 1988

Rei, A., *Have the Baltic Countries Voluntarily Renounced their Freedom?*, New York, 1944

_____, *The Drama of the Baltic Peoples*, Stockholm, 1970

Remeikis, Thomas, *Opposition to Soviet Rule in Lithuania 1945-1980*, Chicago, 1980

Rutter, O., *The New Baltic States*, London, 1925

Sabalionis, Leonas, *Lithuania in Crisis: Nationalism to Communism 1938-1940*, Bloomington, 1972

Sadunaite, Nijole, *Radiance in the Gulag*, Manassas, 1987

Sapoka, Adolfas, *Lithuania Through the Ages*, Muenchen, 1948

_____,*Vilnius in the Life of Lithuania,* Toronto, 1962

Senn, Alfred Erich, *The Emergence of Modern Lithuania*, Toronto, 1962

_____, *Lithuania Awakening,* 1990

_____, *Crisis in Lithuania, January 1991*, Chicago, 1991

Silas, Algirdas J. (editor), *Lithuanian Independence: The U.S. Government Response 1990-1991*, Chicago, 1991

Silbajoris, Rimvydas (editor), *Mind Against the Wall: Essays on Lithuanian Culture under Soviet Occupation*, Chicago, 1983

Sliupas, Jonas, *Essays on the Past, Present and Future of Lithuania*, Stockholm, 1928

Stukas, PhD, Jack J., *Awakening Lithuania, Chicago, 1966*

Suziedelis, Simas (editor), *Encyclopedia Lituanica* (six volumes), Boston, 1970-1978

_____, Saulius, Dr., *The Sword and the Cross: A History of the Church in Lithuania*, Huntington, 1988

Swettenham, J.A., *The Tragedy of the Baltic States*, London, 1952

Tarulis, A.N., *Soviet Policy Toward the Baltic States 1918-1940*, South Bend, 1959

Tauras, K.V., *Guerilla Warfare on the Amber Coast*, New York, 1962

Tautvaisa, H., *Cemetery of Nations in the Siberian Tundra*, The Lithuanian Social Democratic Union of America

Trevor-Roper, Hugh (editor), *The Age of Expansion: Europe and the World 1559-1660*, New York, 1968

Valiukas, L., *Lithuania, Land of Heroes*, Los Angeles, 1962

Valiunas, J.K., *Serving Lithuania*, Southampton, 1988

Vardys, Stanley, *Lithuania Under the Soviets: Portrait of a Nation 1940-65*, New York, 1965

_____, *Captive Lithuania 1944-1962*, New York, 1964

_____, *The Catholic Church, Dissent and Nationality in Soviet Lithuania*, Boulder, 1978

Von Rauch, Georg, *The Baltic States: The Years of Independence 1917-1940*, London, 1970

Walker, Martin, *The Waking Giant*, New York, 1986

Zinkus, Jonas (editor), *Lithuania: An Encyclopedic Survey*, Vilnius, 1986

Zumbakis, S. Paul (editor), *Lithuanian Independence -- the Re-establishment of the Rule of Law*, Chicago, 1990

Val Ramonis is Executive Director
and Curator of the Balzekas Museum
of Lithuanian Culture in Chicago. He
is the author of numerous articles on
history and art.